T0381035

DOCTRINE MAN

AND THE REASON WE BAPTIZE

MEAGHAN F. BEEK

WestBow Press books may be ordered through booksellers or by contacting:

WestBow Press
A Division of Thomas Nelson & Zondervan
1663 Liberty Drive
Bloomington, IN 47403
www.westbowpress.com
1 (866) 928-1240

Interior image Credit: Meaghan Beek, Jenny Turner

Scripture quotations are taken from the King James Version of the Bible.

ISBN: 978-1-9736-6728-5 (sc)
ISBN: 978-1-9736-6729-2 (e)

Library of Congress Control Number: 2019908588

Print information available on the last page.

WestBow Press rev. date: 7/15/2019

WestBow
PRESS®
A DIVISION OF THOMAS NELSON
& ZONDERVAN

DEDICATION

This Bible study is dedicated to Brother Jonathan Follmer, who also inspired the creation of the Character Doctrine man.

Also the Harvest Bible College of Glasgow,
which allowed me to grow in God.

CONTENTS

HOW TO USE THIS STUDY

This Bible Study can be used for all ages, you can split this into four small lessons for younger children who have shorter attention spans, in a classroom setting, or even do it as a one-hour Bible study.

There are five parts to this Bible study, the first part is an instruction manual for the person teaching, it's a guide on what the Bible study pertains. You will find scriptures, discussion points and activities to use.

The second part is a quiz section, one for each part of the study. The quiz is split into three sections, easy, intermediate and an additional bonus question.

The third section is made of coloring pages, you may wish to give the younger ones this to draw their attention, or as homework. You may also wish to use them in a classroom setting as an activity.

The fourth section is the study which the student will be following, these are simple cartoons that follow the study, in the teacher's manual section you will notice that it will say turn to Picture One, Three, Four etc… this is referring to the number in the bottom right hand side of the image.

The fifth and final section is a completion certificate, you may wish to present the student upon completing the study, as a sign of accomplishment and knowing the reason for baptism.

NOTES

_____

_____

_____

_____

DOCTRINE MAN: WHY WE GET BAPTIZED

By day Mr. Moor is a teacher at a Bible college, but by night he is Doctrine Man. He is a superhero dedicated to teaching the Word of God, which is sharper than any two-edged sword, to bring knowledge and love to the world. Doctrine Man can travel back in time to witness the history of the Bible and all the events that happened in the past.

In this adventure, we travel back in time to the formation of the universe and onwards towards our present. Following the ripple effect of Sin, we see how our choices have changed the world in good and bad ways.

So, let's get started and follow the adventures of Doctrine Man.
(Look at Picture One)

NOTES

PART ONE: IN THE BEGINNING:

To find out why we baptise people, we must start at the beginning. In the beginning there was God and, according to the book of John (1:1-3 KJV) in the Bible, "In the beginning was the Word, and the Word was with God, and the Word was God. The same was in the beginning with God. All things were made by him; and without him was not any thing made that was made." Also the first book in the Bible, "Genesis", states that "In the beginning God created the Heavens and the Earth."

-Have your student repeat the scriptures as a memory verse.

It took God 6 days to create everything: (Turn to Picture Two)

Day 1: He made Heaven and Earth; He separated the Dark from the Light. (Genesis 1:1)

Day 2: He created the sky and the sea. (Genesis 1:6)

Day 3: He separated the dry land from the sea and He made the plants and the trees. (Genesis 1:9)

Day 4: He made the moon and the stars, He made the seasons. (Genesis 1:14-19)

Day 5: He made the birds and the fish. (Genesis 1:20)

Day 6: He made the animals, the creeping things (Genesis 1:24) and then He made man (Genesis 1:26)

NOTES

_____
_____
_____
_____

On the seventh day God rested and looked at all His creation and He liked what He saw. God then gave Adam dominion (the right to rule) over all things, and even created a woman for Adam called Eve.

Eve was created after Adam. She was made with the use of Adams rib, God gave Eve to Adam in Genesis 2:23: 'And Adam said, this is now bone of my bones, and flesh of my flesh: she shall be called Woman, because she was taken out of Man'.

Eve was the first person to sin in the Garden of Eden. A serpent tempted her and Eve gave into that temptation and disobeyed God. Adam was the second, he disobeyed God's only rule in the garden. Genesis 3:1-3:6. (Turn to Picture Three)

In the Garden of Eden where Adam and Eve lived, God said to Adam the one thing he was not to do, was not to eat the fruit of the Tree of Knowledge of good and evil, and if Adam did eat the fruit, he would die.

Eve was created after Adam she was made with the use of Adams spare rib, God gave Eve to Adam Genesis 2:23 KJV says 'And Adam said, this is now bone of my bones, and flesh of my flesh: she shall be called Woman, because she was taken out of Man'. Eve was the first person to sin; in the Garden of Eden a serpent tempted Eve and Eve gave into that temptation and disobeyed God. (Turn to picture four)

Genesis 3:1-3:6. KJV "Now the serpent was more subtle than any beast of the field which the LORD God had made. And he said unto the woman, Yea, hath God said, Ye shall not eat of every tree of the garden? And the woman said unto the serpent, We may eat of the fruit of the trees of the garden: But of the fruit of the tree which *is* in the midst of the garden, God hath said, Ye shall not eat of it, neither shall ye touch it, lest ye die. And the serpent said unto the woman, Ye shall not surely die: For God doth know that in the

NOTES
_____
_____
_____
_____

day ye eat thereof, then your eyes shall be opened, and ye shall be as gods, knowing good and evil. And when the woman saw that the tree *was* good for food, and that it *was* pleasant to the eyes, and a tree to be desired to make *one* wise, she took of the fruit thereof, and did eat, and gave also unto her husband with her; and he did eat."

When Eve gave Adam the fruit, it was not until Adam sinned, and ate of the fruit that Man had disobeyed What God had told them not to do. Both eyes were opened and Adam and Eve covered themselves with fig leaves which are very large leaves so they were well covered. When they heard the voice of God, they tried to hide but you cannot hide from God.

They disobeyed God and so they were punished. (relate to the person in whom you are giving this study to, discuss, how for every action there is a reaction, and how when we do something wrong there have consequences. For example, if we something wrong we get grounded or some sort of task, that is what happened to Adam and Eve). When Adam and Eve were in the garden, they did not have to hunt, grow things or do anything, for God supplied everything, but man was cursed and made to till (farm) the ground and hunt. Eve was cursed and told she would go through pain and give birth too many children; she was given the task of populating the earth.

Adam and Eve had to make clothes to cover up the sin of their nakedness, first they used fig leaves, because they are very large, then they had to kill animals. Killing animals provided coverings and food (Blood was shed to cover up sin).

NOTES

_____
_____
_____
_____

3

PART TWO: THE RIPPLE OF SIN:

When we sin or disobey God, we cause a ripple effect. Take for example lying, it takes one lie to destroy someone's life. It takes a lie to cover up a lie, and the more you lie, the more you must make up, but the truth will set you free (John 8:32). Ralph Reynolds, in the book 'Cry of the Unborn', states that "there is no such thing as partial truth, partial obedience is disobedience and partial truth is a lie, two wrongs don't make a right and two lies never make a truth". By disobeying God, Adam and Eve created suffering, by their own hand and by the nature of their original sin: their son Cain killed his brother Able, because Ables death was a worthy sacrifice and it pleased God (Genesis 4:8). (Turn to Picture Five),

-Try filling a bowl with water and have the person in whom you are giving the Bible study throw a stone or an item into the bowl, use this to illustrate the effect of a ripple.

Adam's sin had a ripple effect Jesus' grace stopped it.

God still loved man so he gave us a way to be saved it says in John 3:16: "For God so loved the world, that He gave His only begotten Son, that whosoever believeth in Him should not perish, but have everlasting life."

NOTES
_____
_____
_____
_____

(Turn to Picture Six) In the years after Adam and Eve left Eden, sin ran wild in the world. Among all the sin there was one man who found favor in God's eyes, you can find this in Genesis 6:7 – 12 (the story of Noah, take this time if you wish to tell them the full story of Noah and his family). God told Noah to build an ark to make it out of Gopher wood, make rooms and seal them, he should make it 100 cubits long, 50 cubits wide, and 30 cubits high.

God sent animals to go in the ark, He sent two of every animal, and seven of the clean animals (the ones you eat) like cows and sheep, this was so that God could repopulate the world and Noah and his family would not starve. Noah had a wife and three sons: Ham, Shem and Japheth and they all had wives.

(Turn to Picture Seven) God promised that he would never wipe out the earth with a flood ever again and to show that he made a promise he gave us a rainbow in the sky, and that is why we have rainbows, God gave us them to ensure us when it rains that He is not going to flood the whole world. A rainbow can only be made by white light yet there is none in the sky especially when it rains. This is a miracle from God.

(Turn to Picture Eight) Many years after Noah there were two cities' called Sodom and Gomorrah. These two cities were filled with sin, people stealing and lying and doing all sorts of things that are wrong, this angered God. God told Abraham that He was going to wipe out the cities, but Abraham didn't want God to destroy the cities, so he told the Lord if there be Just one person in the city that is good in any way would he spare the city? And the Lord said he would and there was one, Lot, so the Lord went to Lot and told him to leave the city and not to look back, so Lot got his family grabbed their things and left, but while they were leaving Lot's wife turned around, because she disobeyed by looking back, she was turned to a pillar of salt.

NOTES

_____

_____

_____

_____

God destroyed Sodom and Gomorrah with fire and brimstone, burning the city to the ground, and getting rid of the sin in that area. The sin was still spreading, and God had to bring judgment in a lot of places, like in the city of Nineveh, unlike Sodom and Gomorrah, Nineveh repented, and God spared them. Years later the people of Nineveh turned back to their sin and God did destroy them.

God has given us an escape from having sin dwelling in us and that is repentance. Repentance is the act of asking God for forgiveness and not returning to sin and this makes Him happy, but if we return to sin God does not like.

-Discuss with your student if someone had sinned against them or done something hurtful towards them. If that person had turned around and changed their ways, would they forgive them? Then ask, if they had wronged someone or hurt them, would they want forgiveness?

NOTES

_____
_____
_____
_____

PART THREE: JESUS IS SALVATION:

Sin in the world is still spreading, but God gave us hope and a way to be rid of our sin (Turn to Picture Nine).

In the Old Testament a Prophet called Isaiah said (Isaiah 9:6) 'For unto us a child is born, unto us a son is given: and the Government shall be upon his shoulder: and his name shall be called Wonderful, Counsellor, the mighty God, the everlasting Father, the Prince of Peace'. This was said 400 years before the birth of Jesus; God said, "I will send a messiah to save you all"; this was a prophecy (A message from God about the future).

The birth of Jesus was the best thing to happen to us, God went to Mary and she became pregnant even though she was a virgin and not married, she was chosen to be the mother of Jesus, God robed in flesh.

(Turn to picture 10) Many years later when Jesus became a man, he set the example of how to be born again in the eyes of God. Jesus was baptized, Jesus lived by *examples*, and he practiced what he preached. The example of Jesus being baptized is found in John 1:29 -33. But it wasn't until he died that his blood was shed, and we were able to be baptized for the remission of our sins.

The Jewish people did not believe Jesus was the son of God. The Pharisee, who were like the Jewish version of a policeman, thought Jesus was breaking the Law, so they had Jesus arrested and asked the Romans to execute him.

Jesus was beaten, humiliated and hung on a crucifix for the sins of many. (John 3:16) 'For God so loved the world, that he gave his only begotten Son, that whosoever believeth in him should not perish, but have everlasting life'.

NOTES
_____
_____
_____
_____

(Turn to Picture Eleven) When Jesus was put on the cross a sign was placed above Jesus's head: (John 19:19-20) 'And Pilate wrote a title, and put it on the cross. And the writing was JESUS OF NAZARETH THE KING OF THE JEWS. This title was then read by many of the Jews; for the place where Jesus was crucified was nigh to the city, and it was written in Hebrew, and Greek, and Latin.' That day is the day Jesus died for our sins.

-As an activity you could have your student translate "JESUS OF NAZARETH THE KING OF THE JEWS" into the different languages to hear what they sound and look like or, for younger students, you could have them draw the empty cross with the writing on it.

(Turn to Picture Twelve) Jesus was taken from the cross and placed in a tomb. The tomb belonged to a man called Joseph (not the step father of Jesus) (Luke 23:50, 52-53): 'And, behold, there was a man named Joseph, a counsellor; and he was a good man, and just: This man went unto Pilate, and begged the body of Jesus. And he took it down, and wrapped it in linen, and laid it in a sepulchre that was hewn in stone, wherein never man before was laid.'

Jesus lay in the tomb for three days but on the third day a group of women went to the tomb, (Luke 24:10): 'It was Mary Magdalene and Joanna, and Mary the mother of James, and other women that were with them, which told these things unto the apostles but they found it empty.' It is also mentioned in Mark 16:1:

'When they arrived at the tomb the stone was rolled away and an angel was placed inside telling the women that Jesus was there no more he had risen and that they should tell the Disciples that he is alive, so that is what they did.'

Jesus rising from the dead was the last step in our salvation. Death, burial and resurrection is the key to our salvation. There are three steps we need to take: The first is dying for our sins; The second is being buried having been baptized in Christ; And finally, being resurrected as a new person.

NOTES
_____
_____
_____
_____

PART FOUR: WHY BAPTISM?

A good analogy to describe the death, burial and resurrection of Jesus is that of an apple tree. When an apple falls, it dies and when it dies the seeds fall onto the ground. If the seed is covered by dirt, it starts to grow and change into a new tree. The apple represents us, we are part of the tree which is the world, and Jesus is the breath of life that blows us out of the tree. When we let God into our life the old flesh (the apple) melts away, only the seeds are left, our heart, our soul, our mind, the things the make us ourselves. Our seeds are buried in the ground and God makes us new, we become better than our old selves, we are not an apple but a tree in God's kingdom.

-Have your student draw an apple on one side of a piece of paper, and then write all the things that were bad about them before they knew Jesus. Then have them draw a tree and write all their blessings on the branches, and things they think are good about themselves. Once they are done, take the apple and tear it up, explain how when you become baptized into the kingdom of God you are a new person and God does not care about who you were, because the old you is buried under the weight of Jesus love and sacrifice.

(Turn to Page Thirteen) The day of Pentecost was a Jewish festival 50 days after the Passover. The day of Pentecost is the last festival of spring, it is a day when you are to drawn close to God and receive the glory to come.

NOTES

_____

_____

_____

_____

Jesus ascended (rose up into the sky) on the day of Pentecost and when the disciples returned to where the upper room, they all started praying as one. That is when God poured out his Holy Spirit, there was a sound like the rushing wind and cloven tongues of fire, (fire that is split) appeared on the heads of the people. When the Holy Ghost filled the people, they spoke in known and unknown languages (also known as tongues) and people thought that they were drunk.

When someone receives the 'Gift of the Holy Ghost' they are part of the way to getting saved, the next thing for them to do is get baptised, but they must know what it means to be baptized, and why are they getting baptized.

God loved Adam and Eve, but their disobedience caused Sin, and God sent himself as Jesus to die, so that we may have life in heaven with Him. He stayed in the tomb for three days and rose. This was to prove that he was God robed in flesh, and to give us the key to salvation.

Teachers, please take the time to ask your student what they have learnt and if they understand what salvation is and why we get baptized.

NOTES
_____
_____
_____
_____

QUIZ BOOK

QUIZ ONE: LESSON 1

Young Learner Quiz:

Question 1: what is the name of the super hero in the Bible study?
Answer: Doctrine Man

Question 2: Who created the world?
Answer: God (Genesis 1:1)

Question 3: What did God create on the sixth day?
Answer: Man

Question 4: What were the names of the first man and woman?
Answer: Adam and Eve

Question 5: Who tricked Eve?
Answer: a serpent

NOTES
_____
_____
_____
_____

Advanced Learner Quiz:

Question 1: Who created the world and give a reference?
Answer: God (Genesis 1:1)

Question 2: What did God create on the last Day?
Answer: Nothing, God rested

Question 3: What was Adam and Eve's Sin?
Answer: Ate the fruit that God told them not to eat.

Question 4: What did Adam and Eve use to cover themselves with?
Answer: Fig leaves.

Question 5: What did the sin of Adam and Eve do?
Answer: Cause a ripple effect of Sin.

Bonus question:

State what was created on each day?
Answer: Day 1 – Light and Darkness; Day 2 - Heaven; Day 3 – Land on Earth, the Seas and all Plants; Day 4 – The Sun, Moon, Stars and Seasons; Day 5 - The Birds and the Fish; Day 6 - Animals and creeping things and finally Adam; Day 7 – on the last day God rested.

NOTES
_____
_____
_____
_____

QUIZ TWO: LESSON 2

Young Learner Quiz:

....

Question 1: What did Adam's sin create?
Answer: A ripple effect.

Question 2: Who built an Ark?
Answer: Noah.

Question 3: How many sons did Noah have?
Answer: Three.

Question 4: What did God put in the sky as a
promise not to flood the earth again?
Answer: A rainbow.

Question 5: What did God do to Sodom and Gomorrah?
Answer: Destroyed them.

NOTES

_____
_____
_____
_____

Advanced Learner Quiz:

Question 1: Name the three sons of Noah.
Answer: Ham, Shem and Japheth

Question 2: What type of wood was the Ark built of?
Answer: gopher wood

Question 3: Who turned into a pillar of salt?
Answer: Lot's wife

Question 4: What did God use to Judge Sodom and Gomorrah?
Answer: Fire and Brimstone

Question 5: What stopped the ripple effect?
Answer: Jesus' Grace

Bonus question:

Question: How many Cubits long was Noah's Ark?
Answer: 100 Cubits

NOTES

QUIZ THREE: LESSON 3

Young Learner Quiz:

Question 1: Who was born in a stable?
Answer: Jesus

Question 2: Who baptized Jesus?
Answer: John the Baptist

Question 3: Who died on the cross?
Answer: Jesus

Question 4: How many people were crucified with Jesus?
Answer: Two

Question 5: What did it say on the Cross above Jesus?
Answer: This is Jesus the King of the Jews

NOTES

Advanced Learner Quiz:

Question 1: How many years were between the
old testaments and the birth of Jesus?
Answer: 400 years

Question 2: Why was Jesus baptized?
Answer: To set an example

Question 3: Who did not believe Jesus was the Messiah?
Answer: The Jews

Question 4: Who did Jesus die for?
Answer: Me and you

Question 5: What were the people who died alongside Jesus?
Answer: Thieves

Bonus question:

Quote John 3:16: "For God so loved the world, that he
gave his only begotten Son, that whosoever believeth in
him should not perish but have everlasting life."

NOTES

_____
_____
_____
_____

QUIZ FOUR: LESSON 4

Young Learner Quiz:

....

Question 1: What appeared above the heads of
the people on the day of Pentecost?
Answer: A clove of fire.

Question 2: Were there women in the upper room?
Answer: Yes.

Question 3: What is the first step of salvation?
Answer: Death/repenting.

Question 4: What is the second step in salvation?
Answer: Burial/baptism.

Question 5: What is the last step in salvation?
Answer: Resurrection/new life in Christ.

NOTES

_____

_____

_____

_____

Advanced learner Quiz:

Question 1: What were the people in the upper room accused of being?
Answer: Drunk

Question 2: What appeared above the heads of
the people on the day of Pentecost?
Answer: A clove of fire.

Question 3: What is the first step of salvation?
Answer: Death/repenting.

Question 4: What is the second step in salvation?
Answer: Burial/baptism.

Question 5: What is the last step in salvation?
Answer: Resurrection/new life in Christ.

Bonus question:

What have you learnt about salvation and what being baptised means?

NOTES
_____
_____
_____
_____

ACTIVITY PAGES

God rested...Zzz

②

Black and white image of the days of creation

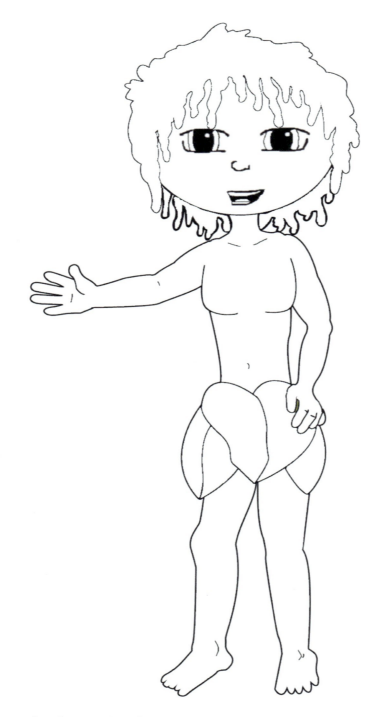

Black and white coloring image of Adam

Black and white coloring image of Eve

NOTES

_____
_____
_____
_____

Black and White image of Doctrine Man

Black and white image of an angel

NOTES

PICTURE BIBLE STUDY

Doctrine Man by day and night

The 6 days of creation

Adam and Eve talking to Doctrine man

Eve talking

A ripple

Noah's ark

Rainbow

NOTES
_____
_____
_____
_____

Doctrine man standing outside Sodom and Gomorrah

Christmas night

Jesus being baptised

Jesus on the cross

Stone rolled away

Fire on people's heads

Certificate of Completion

THIS ACKNOWLEDGES THAT

HAS COMPLETED THE DOCTRINE MAN AND WHY WE BAPTIZE BIBLE STUDY

DATE

TEACHER

Printed in the United States
By Bookmasters